REDEMPTIVE SUFFERING

Sanctified by Suffering:

Understanding suffering from the life of Fr. Sylvester

By

Chioma Okolia

Published by The Book Chief Publishing House 2025

(a trademark under Lydian Group Ltd)
Suite 2A, Blackthorn House, St Paul's Square,
Birmingham, B3 1RL
www.thebookchief.com

ISBN: 978-1-917592-07-9

Book Cover Design: The Book Chief / Abu Baker Javed
Editing / Formatting: The Book Chief
Consultation / Publishing: Sharon Brown

Published by The Book Chief

Disclaimer on Personal Data and Identifiability

This book includes references to individuals who have played meaningful roles in the author's life and experiences. In order to respect personal privacy and comply with data protection principles, only first names have been used throughout the text unless prior consent has been explicitly obtained or the information is already publicly available.

No sensitive personal data (such as full names, religious affiliations, medical details, or locations) has been intentionally published without consent. Any resemblance to actual persons, living or deceased, is either coincidental or has been rendered anonymous to protect the individual's privacy.

The author and publisher have taken reasonable steps to anonymise non-essential identifying details where consent has not been secured. If any person believes they have been identified and wishes to discuss the content, request removal or redaction in future editions, they are encouraged to contact the publisher at **sharon@thebookchief.com**

This publication is intended as a reflective and spiritual account. It is not meant to infringe on anyone's privacy or legal rights.

Charities

A portion of the proceeds from every copy sold of this book will go towards supporting the incredible work of the following charities. Please note that it is at the author's discretion to change the selected charities and to determine the duration for which donations from book sales will be made.

Great Ormond Street Hospital:

Supporting seriously ill children and their families, Great Ormond Street Hospital helps fund life-saving research, advanced medical equipment, and family support services, ensuring every child receives the best possible care.

Macmillan Cancer Support:

A UK leading charity offering emotional, practical, and financial support to people affected by cancer. They provide expert information, specialist nurses, and community services, helping individuals live as fully as possible from diagnosis through treatment and beyond.

This will be alternated with similar charities in Nigeria-a country close to our hearts.

By purchasing this book, you're not just supporting the author, you're helping to make a difference in the lives of others. THANK YOU.

Table Of Contents

About the Book

The reality of suffering and the appropriate response to it when it happens to us, calls for a deep reflection even though it could be difficult. There are times when the suffering is another's and when we are not the ones who suffer directly.

In this, the Christian response is exemplified in the story of the Good Samaritan. We are not allowed to *"pass by on the other side"* with the indifference exhibited by the Priest and Levite. Our sensitivity to the sufferings of others must move us to compassion for the suffering person.

The presence of suffering in the world today should unleash the love and compassion inherent in every human heart and move everyone to actions that will ameliorate and ultimately end the causes of suffering. The revelation of the salvific meaning of suffering counteracts the prevailing attitude of passivity.

The Gospel negates passivity in the face of suffering. This book treats suffering as something that happens to everyone, using faith and reason to answer the question of why bad things happen to good people.

Dedication

Dedicated to those going through very severe illnesses.

This is to encourage you that you are not alone in this journey.

Acknowledgement

This is a great opportunity to thank all those who have helped me in the amazing feat of publishing this book.

My sincerest appreciation goes to Fr. Benedict Ashade who used his professional, creative and innovative experiences to contribute great ideas which have made this book a success.

Many thanks to my dearest mum, Chibuzo, my brothers Jideofo and Chukwuemeka together with his wife Ifeyinwa, my nephew Jomike and my niece Kaima who have continuously encouraged and supported me towards the completion of this book.

I would equally like to thank my religious mentors Fr. Patrick Feyisetan, Fr. Albert Ofere, Fr. Gregory Verissimo and my friends Kingsley, Oladewa, Ikana, Emmanuel, Kadi, and my colleagues at work who relentlessly stood by me in one of the most heartbreaking moments of my life.

A special and heartfelt thanks to the Lead Publishing Coordinator and my brother, Jide Okolia, who made it his responsibility that this story and teachings be told to a far greater audience. His guidance and expertise steered the entire decision-making process for this book and his leadership ensured every element aligned seamlessly, bringing the author’s vision to life with care and precision.

Preface

Sometimes in our lives as humans, we feel neglected or forgotten by our friends, close relatives and, in most cases, by God.

We go to church every Sunday, attend Masses during the week and even do all that God requires us to do as Christians, yet at our lowest moments in life, we call upon HIM and it seems as though HE is far away from us or maybe even close to us, but not paying attention to our cries, especially when we are desperate for answers and solutions.

We tend to lose hope easily, forgetting that with hope, there is life, either on earth or life after death. This book, on the one hand, tries to examine the reality of suffering in human existence, which may include severe illnesses, hardship, or even the death of our loved ones, and on the other hand, it encourages Christians to understand suffering from a redemptive point of view, which eventually leads to our freedom in the end, knowing that our creator has no other intentions for us but to redeem us from evil.

Reflecting deeply on my experience with Fr. Sylvester and the impact my relationship with him as my Spiritual Director had on my life, it seemed adequate to put down a few words of reflection on the impact of my experience of his sufferings, which has greatly shaped my understanding of life and human relationships and has strengthened my faith.

This book, therefore, does not claim to be a scholarly attempt but a personal reflection of my experience and moments in life, be it: joy and sadness, comfort and pain, courage and fortitude, weakness and hope.

How it all started

Late January 2018, I visited Fr. Sylvester, fondly called 'Fr. Sly', with two other priests, after being informed of the terminal illness he was battling with. On getting to his parish, I felt overwhelmed and was close to tears, but I had to be strong for him, by encouraging him. Fr. Sylvester and I excused ourselves and took a walk in the neighbourhood and we had so much to talk about and laugh over, that no one would have known, if you had not physically met him that he was battling with an illness. He had lost a lot of weight but was still full of life and had a wonderful charisma.

Whilst we were taking a walk, he mentioned the stage of his health condition and that he would be returning back to Nigeria the following month, as he did not have long to live and would want nothing more than being surrounded by his family, especially his mother for his final goodbye. It was the hardest thing I had ever had to deal with, knowing that I was never going to see him again once he returned to Nigeria.

On the 4th of February whilst he was at the airport en route to Nigeria, he called me to say his goodbye. When he arrived in Nigeria, Fr. Sylvester was taken to University College Hospital (UCH)

Ibadan, and I lost direct contact with him. At this time, I communicated with some of his priest friends who gave me updates on his health and that he was deteriorating fast.

On the night of 27th March 2018, I wasn't in a good state of mind and decided to go to bed early. Fr. Sylvester appeared to me that night in my dream and as usual was very chatty and smiling. He told me he was going somewhere and would like a favour from me. I kept asking, *"Where are you?"* He just kept smiling and then I asked, *"What is the favour?"* He said, *"I would like you to write a book about a 'COHEN'."*

I knew people who go by the name COHEN as their surname, but never knew the meaning. Just after he told me the favour he wanted, he started walking towards a deserted area and told me not to follow him. I kept screaming his name asking him to wait for me, but I realised the more I ran to catch up with him, the more he doubled his footsteps. I kept chasing after him without any success. Just as I was about to catch up with him, there was a footbridge that led across the river, and he quickly walked across the bridge to the other side and as I approached the bridge, it collapsed and he disappeared. I woke up very confused, wondering what the message meant.

The following day on the 28th of March 2018, I got a call from one of his priest friends informing me of his demise. The news was so devastating. I seized the opportunity to discuss the dream I had the day before with the priest and informed him that I was asked to write a book about a 'COHEN'. The priest then told me that 'COHEN' is of Hebrew origin meaning 'Priest' and thereafter encouraged me to go ahead and write a book about his final days which most likely was the message Fr. Sylvester was trying to pass on. Hence, this has prompted me to write this book in his honour and donate some of the proceeds to charity.

Chapter One

The Person of Fr. Sylvester

Reverend Father Sylvester Nwannedimma Ogbogu was a 45-year-old Society of African Missions (S.M.A.) priest when he returned to his creator.

The cancer, the Ibusa-born priest endured defied treatments and in the end, chemotherapy was not enough remedy. Although the therapy indicated manifestations of recuperation, a relapse brought to an end a life that will forever typify to the people who took this journey with Fr. Sylvester, a glimpse into the mystery of life and death, joy in suffering and strength of grace to witness to God even in the event of illness and ultimately in death.

From his birth on 1st September, 1972, to his glorious passing to eternity in March 2018, Fr. Sylvester was a gift to those who shared his life.

To the family of Mr and Mrs Ogbogu, he was the third child and first son. He was baptised in 1986 while living with his aunt in Lagos. He joined the 'Altar Boys' Association in the same year, where his interest in service to God and the Church bloomed.

Added to this was his position as a lector, which offered young Sylvester the responsibility of proclaiming the Good News at liturgical celebrations.

All these meant he was a regular at daily masses in the mornings and evenings. This did not go down well with his aunt and her children. Nonetheless, their complaints about his frequency of church activities were insufficient to deter the young man from serving God within the context of the mass and other church functions.

Sylvester also fought internal battles, struggling to overcome his timidity and nervousness. He knew that his utmost desire for God in the Catholic priesthood would require him to answer God's call to the Holy altar of sacrifice and that he had to overcome these fears. In these struggles, he put his faith in God, believing that if he was really called by God, then the Spirit would furnish him with the courage and strength to carry on over and above his timidity and nervousness.

His zeal for the service of God and humanity was apparent when he began his journey to the priesthood with the S.M.A. in 1995. His first port of call was the S.M.A. House of Formation in Bodija, Ibadan, Nigeria. He was next at the Saints Peter and Paul Major Seminary, Ibadan, Nigeria, from October 1995 to June 1999 for his studies in Philosophy. There, he obtained his Bachelors in Philosophy which was a pivotal step in his priestly training. This training continued in the Republic of Benin at the International Spiritual Year Centre of the S.M.A. in Calavi. From October 1991 to June 2000, he joined other young men for intense discernment of his vocation.

The S.M.A. formation structure often combined this process with a period of missionary experience to provide the prospective candidate for the priesthood with hands-on, practical discernment and experience of the S.M.A.'s life and mission.

At the end of the training, he took his first oath as a temporary member of the Society of African Missions on 25th June, 2000. In October of the same year, in keeping with the S.M.A. formation structure, Sylvester was sent to Côte d'Ivoire for missionary experience.

To consolidate his decision to continue on the journey of the Catholic priesthood, he worked in the Borotu-Koro parish in the diocese of Odienné from October 2000 to June 2001. After that, firm in his desire to continue to the priesthood, he was asked to return to the same S.M.A. House of Formation in Ibadan, Nigeria and proceed with his studies in Theology at the SS. Peter and Paul Seminary in Bodija, Ibadan, as well.

On 7th December 2004, Sylvester took his final vows and became a permanent member of the S.M.A. His priestly ordination came the following year as he was raised to the order of the priesthood on the 2nd of July, 2005.

In October of the same year, Fr. Sylvester Ogbogu, S.M.A., resumed his first appointment as a missionary priest in Zambia, working in the Ndola Diocese. He spent six (6) productive years in the Zambian missionary fields, where he was greatly esteemed by his S.M.A. confreres and the people of God whom he served in the parish.

His warm and welcoming presence was also felt by those who encountered him while he was involved in Mission Appeals for the S.M.A. British Province, first from the S.M.A. House in New

Barnet and later from the new S.M.A. House in West London. He had been sent on these Appeals as a seconded Member of the S.M.A. British Province beginning in September 2011.

He brought this selfless character to his mission and work in God's vineyard. Those who encountered him testified that a Christ-like spirit encased his ministry as a priest, and this quality endeared many to him. Even in the lowest points of his treatments and therapies, when the ailment took a hefty toll on his physical, psychological, and spiritual constitution, Fr. Sylvester maintained a smiling disposition.

It was he who encouraged sympathisers, friends and family alike, to take consolation in the eternal goodness of the Almighty in whose hands rested the power of life and death.

The example of Fr. Sylvester's absolute submission to the will of God astounded not just a few. Confreres, family and friends marvelled at how well he took his condition and wondered at the peace he radiated while suffering what they knew was a debilitating illness.

They remember him fondly as never once dismayed about what he endured nor ever disheartened when he relapsed and resigned to God's holy will.

He wished to see his mother before returning to his Maker. For this, he was flown back to Nigeria and allowed time to see her.

There was no better confirmation of God's hand working in Fr. Sylvester's life than the fact that the one who joyfully offered all his trials and tribulations to God in conjunction with the passion and sufferings of Christ breathed his last during the celebrations of the most important period of the Church's calendar: **Holy Week**, when the Church commemorates the sufferings and price it took to win us our salvation. It's culminated in a life that elevated human suffering to the level of a life-giving sacrifice and, in so doing, taught us a lesson in redemptive suffering.

Fr. Sylvester's illness and his eventual passing, raises questions that have troubled the minds of Christians and some non-Christians alike about the nature of an Almighty and all-loving God.

This priest who administered the sacraments to others, especially to the sick, this shepherd who suffered with his flock, this soul-physician who cared for the infirm had no one else to turn to when his situation took a turn for the worse but God Himself. Yet this God to whom the priest dedicated a life of denial and service looked on as he worsened, suffered and died.

How can that be the act of a loving Being?

What would it have cost the omnipotent God to immediately heal his servant?

Is there something missing in our knowledge of God, of suffering and death?

It is to provide answers to these queries that this piece employs the use of critical reflection and sacred scriptures in order to present the redemptive aspect of suffering.

Chapter Two

The Reality of Suffering in Human Existence

It is a known fact that no one likes to suffer or even pray for it, but in this world, in our societies, in our communities, and in our families, we come in contact directly or indirectly with different forms of human suffering.

Some suffer natural disasters and the consequent pains they bring; for others, degrading human conditions such as malnutrition, hunger, wars, violence, abuse of human rights, oppression, marginalisation, dehumanisation and so on. For some of these instances of suffering, there could be remedies, but for some, there may not be any. It would seem that when there are remedies available, human beings find it easier to pull through their difficult moments, but when there is none available, the possibility of submitting to despair is great. When natural disasters happen, who is to blame for them? When the power of science also becomes inadequate to remedy grave diseases, could it be that the scientists have not done enough to better the lot of the world?

In coming to terms with the problem of the presence of suffering in the world and the strongly held Christian position about an ever-benevolent God, Christian and non-Christian apologists alike have vehemently debated for and against that Christian position.

These arguments are hinged on the seeming illogicality in conceding that a benign Deity will allow malevolence to come to His faithful servants, as is evident in the world today when allegedly He is omnipotent enough to prevent it. This throws in a challenge that asks if this is a concession to an inherent lack of God's abilities. Queries that are sure to arise in this and typical situations hinge on the nature of this Almighty and omnipotent God who will consent to the suffering of his beloved children, to the pains and trials of the innocent and the faithful and especially to his priests like Fr. Sylvester Ogbogu.

If God is "Father" and "Almighty", why does He allow evil and suffering in the world?

If God is all-powerful and truly seeks our good, then why does He allow bad things to happen to people, even good people like Fr. Sylvester?

Why does He allow all the suffering we experience in this life if He truly loves us?

Scriptural basis of suffering, life and death

The prevalent view of suffering and death, which is devoid of divine significance, views suffering through the lenses of human agency and material *'wisdom'*. As a consequence, suffering has little or no meaning.

At the other end of this spectrum is the conventional African sense that sees suffering from the prism of a pragmatic religious formula where all blessings are seen as evidence of goodness and righteousness, with all suffering witnessed to unrighteousness and punishment for evil. In neither of these two extremes can be situated the redemptive character of trials and tribulations. That is why we turn to the scriptures for clarification on that basis.

In St. Paul's letter to the Romans, we come to terms with the foundational understanding of the origins of suffering and death in the world. It is a consequence of sin. The Apostle writes in **(Romans 6:23)** *"For the wages of sin is death."* With the free choice of our first parents in the Garden of Eden, sin entered into the world. With it came suffering and death, both physical and spiritual.

The Catechism of the Catholic Church (1997) builds on this scriptural basis to explain that as a result of original sin, human nature is weakened in its powers, subject to ignorance, suffering, and the domination of death, and is inclined to sin. This will be explored further in the section that treats suffering from a theological perspective.

Though some of the sources of our suffering pertain to personal sin and are often the consequences of our sinful actions, the innocent also suffer. All these are repercussions of sin entering the world.

One of the most iconic representations of the suffering of the innocent in the Old Testament is Job. For a man described as one who *"feared God and avoided evil"* and who the Bible noted to be *"blameless and upright"*, he had to endure a great deal of pain and suffering when everything he held dear, and for which he had laboured, went up in smoke leaving him a broken man.

It is a testament to his faith and a forecast to the example of the Lamb of God that at the lowest of his brokenness, Job could still proclaim with the fervour of his faith that, *"I know that my Redeemer lives and that he will at last stand forth upon the dust; whom I shall see: my own eyes, not another's, shall behold him, and from my flesh I shall see God; my inmost being is consumed with longing."* **(Job 19:25-27).**

The theology of retribution and recompense, which attributes all blessings as evidence of goodness and righteousness while all suffering as proof of unrighteousness and sin was crystallised in the admonition of Job's friends, *"Repent of your sins so God can forgive you and so restore your prosperity."* ***(Job 22:23).*** Satan was the origin of the effects Job suffered in the course of Satan's desires to reach his objective to turn a righteous man (Job) against a just God.

This objective – founded on Satan's query, *"Is it love or self-satisfying greed that motivates a person's righteousness and leads such a person to fear God and keep away from sin?"* – was behind all that Satan inflicted on Job. Were Job to agree that he served God for *"something"*, Satan would have proved his case in the ‘court of heaven’.

In reflecting on the Book of Job, we see that the lesson Job learns was, what was of pivotal importance in the journey of salvation was God's grace rather than any individual's piety, which runs contrary to the prevailing *"prosperity gospel"*.

Though we see that the book describes a strongly-held tradition of Ancient Israelites and others of the Near East who explained suffering under the rubric of retribution or recompense theology, it could also have been directly referring to some preachers today and their materialistic conception of suffering, trials and tribulations.

In Isaiah's writings, we see foretold the suffering of the promised Messiah when he prophesied, *"He was spurned and avoided by men, a man of suffering, accustomed to infirmity"*...yet it was our infirmities that he bore, our sufferings that he endured...but he was pierced for our offences, crushed for our sins*..."Through suffering, my servant shall justify many and their guilt he shall bear...and he shall take away the sins of many and win pardon for their offences."* ***(Isaiah 53:3, 4, 5, 11, 12).***

Here, we see how suffering can bring about salvation, the suffering of one for the salvation of the many. But that is the salvific suffering of Christ. It is highlighted here to call to mind the redemptive quality of suffering. Every other suffering that is borne in union with it gains from its redemptive qualities and joins in the sacrificial objective of that passion and death on Calvary that brought forth our redemption.

Elisha's ministry prefigured Jesus's salvific mission, as the prophet was an instrument of God's healing and raising from the dead. He instructed the Syrian commander, Naaman, to wash seven times in Jordan. When Naaman did, he was healed of the leprosy he had suffered, leading him to proclaim, *"Now, I know that there is no God in all the earth except in Israel."* ***(2 Kings 5:15).***

Before that, in ***(Kings 2:4)***, Elisha raised the dead child of a woman by stretching himself over the child and breathing into the child's mouth. Here, we see healing and bringing back to life, all within the prophetic ministry of Elisha, prefiguring the power over suffering and death that was to come with the coming of the Son of man, the Messiah.

These candid examples from scripture tell of the manifestation of God's glory as he conquers illness and death, just as they show that he allows death for this glory as well. All things (life, suffering, illness, death) work together for good for those who believe ***(Rom 8:28)***.

That is why the ultimate admonition remains: *"In ALL THINGS give thanks."* ***(1 Thess 5:18)***—not only *"in good things"* or *"in some things"* but *"in ALL things."*

The scriptures also offer us consolation in illness. In ***(James 5:14)***, we find the essential elements of the special sacrament of the Anointing of the Sick:

"Is anyone among you suffering? He should pray. Is anyone in good spirits? He should sing praise. Is anyone among you sick? He should summon the presbyters (priests) of the Church, and they should pray over him and anoint him with oil in the name of the Lord."

St. Paul's notions of suffering

In his writings, the Apostle Paul sees in his experience of suffering, a participation in salvation, especially the passion, death and resurrection of Christ. Paul believes his suffering serves the purpose of making him like Christ as well as being for the sake of Christ. He was happy to have suffered the loss of all things, counting everything as worthless, in order to gain Christ and be found in him without any righteousness of his own and by sharing thus in Christ's suffering to become like him in his death and in that death to attain life. ***(Philippians 3:8-11).***

For Paul, suffering here constituted a participation in the mystery of Christ, in a process that transformed the sufferer into a Christ-like vessel who participates in Christ's passion and death in order to obtain salvation. For to live is Christ and to die is gain. ***(cf. Philippians 1:21)***. In this latter piece, Paul notes that surviving any suffering exhibits the resurrection that he can share with others for their edification, but if he does not survive, if he dies, he shares in the resurrection of Christ himself which ushers him to a union with the Master and presents to those who outlive him an example to follow.

Paul also considered suffering to be a means of sanctification, an instrument to keep pride at bay.

He wrote that *"a thorn"* was given to him in the flesh to harass him and keep him from being too elated, too exalted beyond measure.

He entreated God to allow him to be free of this *"thorn"* but was reminded, *"My grace is sufficient for you, for my power is made perfect in weakness".* This was enough for Paul to declare that, for Christ's sake, he was content with whatever he had to endure: weaknesses, insults, hardships, persecutions, and calamities. He learnt that it was in his weakness that the power of God was manifested in him. ***(2 Cor. 12:7-10).***

Our weakened, infirm and ailing state creates a more pliable foundation on which to build a fortified trust in Christ, as we realise that what we end up accomplishing is not of our own making but for the grace of Christ Jesus working in us. Thus, we grow in humility and sieve out the haughty vice of pride, which can secretly creep into our minds and hearts to turn us away from total submission to God. In this vein, Paul writes that we suffer *"to make us rely, not on ourselves but on God who raises the dead."* ***(2 Cor. 1:9).***

Without grace, seeing the sublimity of suffering as a salvific act is impossible. It is through grace that we can be content with suffering, smile through pain, and welcome death.

It is the efficacy of grace that empowers the one suffering to be an example to those who sympathise with the sufferer. This provides ample witness to the presence of grace that would have submerged Fr. Sylvester. Grace helps us to participate in the salvific act of suffering and to be content with the pain and the hurt, offering it all to the Father in communion with the sacrifice of Christ's passion. Imbued in this grace, a sufferer can claim with Paul in ***(Galatians 2:20),*** *"I have been crucified with Christ (in my sufferings) and it is no longer I who live but Christ who lives in me."*

This faith, thus, emboldens Paul to claim in ***(2 Cor. 4:8-10)*** *"We are afflicted in every way, but not crushed; perplexed, but not driven to despair; persecuted, but not forsaken; struck down, but not destroyed; always carrying in the body the death of Jesus, so that the life of Jesus may also be manifested in our bodies."* Those who knew Fr. Sylvester would read these words with joy kindled in their hearts because it would seem St. Paul was referring to him. Personally, Fr. Sylvester truly embodied the unrelenting spirit of one whose jovial personality in suffering manifested the life of Christ in his body.

As a result of this rekindled hope, we can say with St. Paul on behalf of Fr. Sylvester, that even in suffering, our hope remains steadfast because: *"We rejoice in our sufferings, knowing that suffering produces endurance, and endurance produces character, and character produces hope, and hope does not disappoint us, because God's love has been poured into our hearts through the Holy Spirit which has been given to us."* ***(cf. Rom. 5:3-5).***

The paradoxical nature of the suffering that typified the sacrifice at Calvary signifies that death now means life. That thing that is a folly to those who are perishing becomes the very power of God to save the perishing. The agency of this manifestly salvific suffering of Christ carries its power to make it beneficial to all of creation.

Hence, when we bear suffering in self-negation and are united to Christ's sacrificial offering of Self, our sufferings gain this agency and make it beneficial to those with whom we are in communion by virtue of our belonging to the same body via baptism. St. Paul makes repeated allusions to this. *"If one part suffers, every part suffers with it; if one part is honoured, every part rejoices with it."* ***(1 Cor. 12:26).*** *"For as we share abundantly in Christ's sufferings, so through Christ, we share abundantly in comfort too."* ***(2 Cor. 1:5).*** *"For while we live, we are always being given up to death for Jesus' sake, so that the life of Jesus may be manifested in our mortal flesh ... knowing that he who raised the Lord Jesus will raise us also with Jesus."* ***(2 Cor. 4:11,14).***

"That I may know Him (Christ) and the power of His Resurrection, and may share His sufferings, becoming like Him in His death, that if possible, I may attain the resurrection from the dead." ***(Phil. 3:10-11)***. *"Now, I rejoice in my sufferings for your sake, and in my flesh, I do my share on behalf of His body, which is the Church, in filling up what is lacking in Christ's afflictions."* ***(Col. 1:24).***

Called to communion

The gospels show us that suffering is an opportunity presented to us, giving us a participatory chance in our future blessedness when we offer our present sufferings, in union with Christ's sufferings, to God in a self-giving sacrifice.

This sacrifice becomes divinely transformed into the greatest opportunity to show God, trust and self-donation, knowing that it will be rewarded a hundredfold without the least futility. This is why when the martyrs were slain for the faith, they rejoiced for being considered worthy to be chosen for martyrdom, to be considered worthy to suffer shame for His name ***(Acts 5:41)***.

Stripped from the gospel, sufferings and trials appear meaninglessly and hopelessly empty of sense. It is in the light of the gospel that we testify to the giftedness of suffering, a gift of the same sort as this present life but by far greater in every sense. It is a chance and an opportunity to give ourselves entirely to God in the greatest possible expression of love as a sacrifice.

Jesus Christ, when he redeemed us with plentiful redemption, took not away the pains and sorrows which in such large proportion are woven together in the web of our mortal life. He transformed them into motives of virtue and occasions of merit and no man can hope for eternal reward unless he follows in the blood-stained footprints of his Saviour.

"If we suffer with Him, we shall also reign with him."

Christ's labours and sufferings, accepted of His own free will, have marvellously sweetened all suffering and all labour, not only by his example but by His grace and the hope held forth of everlasting recompense, has He made pain and grief easier to endure.

"For that which is at present momentary and light of our tribulation, worketh for us above measure exceedingly an eternal weight of glory." ***(Rerum Novarum, 21).***

Chapter Three

Evil, Suffering and Eternal Life

In his epistle, the Apostle John did not mince words when he stated that *"God is love"* **(1 Jn 4:8)**. It is the quality of genuine love to seek the good of the one loved. St. Thomas Aquinas quoted Aristotle as saying, *"To love is to wish the good of someone"* **(Summa Theologica II-I Q.26 a.4)**. Thus, when you love a person, all you want for that person is what is truly good for him or her and what truly and most perfectly makes him or her happy. For God, His love of us is infinitely more than whatever depth of love we can muster for each other. By implication, we can infer that God wants us to have what is good for us and what truly makes us happy.

Does this fly in the face of the reality we witness in life? Does it not make it all the more perplexing and contradictory that we have a God who loves us so much and still we see so much suffering even among those who serve, worship and dedicate their lives to doing the work of this omnipotent God? Again, those often-repeated queries can be put forward here as well: If He is so powerful, and truly seeks our good, then why does He allow the sufferings we experience in life? Suffering that his own servant Fr. Sylvester Ogbogu was not spared of?

This line of questioning has been the major staple of *"The New Reasoning".* The instigators of this new rationalisation, point to these sufferings and evils in the world around us and argue that there cannot be a good God because if there were, He would potently deal with such meaningless, pointless evils and sufferings that afflict humanity. The underlying assumption in the major plank of this argument is, if we cannot see any justification for evil and suffering, there is no reason for it to be seen or it is unreasonable to believe there is one in the first place. This presupposes the instigator's objection, that a Being infinitely greater than ourselves either does not exist or has not revealed His goodness and love to us, and following that line of argument, the objection assumes exactly what it is trying to show.

For these instigators, suffering, evil, tragedy and loss are ultimately meaningless and pointless. To this end, these aspects of life ought to be avoided at all costs. If something good is not the anticipated result, one ought to spare no expense in avoiding evil and suffering.

There is, for the protagonists of this reasoning, the additional despair of seeing no higher meaning or purpose for all the suffering one endures and the evils with which one is beset.

There cannot be any redemptive benefits in any suffering for these instigators. This is the basis for which such protagonists will consider ending a life if for any reasons and all things being equal, there is present suffering without the foreseeable possibility of coming to a quality of life that outweighs that suffering. This is why an instigator like this lends support for euthanasia, the selective killing of the aged, the terminally ill, infants born with Down's Syndrome and others considered incapable of attaining a quality of life that outweighs their suffering.

To tackle this theologically, it is apposite to go back to the very beginning. As St. Paul made obvious in his letter to the Romans, death came into the world through sin. *"Therefore, just as through one-man sin entered into the world, and death through sin, and so death spread to all men, because all sinned ..."* ***(Rom. 5:12***).

Before this became the case, we have a glimpse of the condition of man and nature from Genesis: *"God saw all that He had made, and behold, it was very good."* ***(Gen. 1:31)***

This informs us of the nature of things before *"death came into the world through sin"*. Everything God made was good and they were in harmony, one with the other.

This is how the Catechism of the Catholic Church ***(CCC 373-376)*** describes this harmony:

> The first man was not only created good, but was also established in friendship with his Creator and in harmony with himself and with the creation around him, in a state that would be surpassed only by the glory of the new creation in Christ ... Our first parents, Adam and Eve, were constituted in an original *"state of holiness and justice"*. This grace of original holiness was *"to share in ... divine life"*. By the radiance of this grace all dimensions of man's life were confirmed. As long as he remained in the divine intimacy, man would not have to suffer or die. The inner harmony of the human person, the harmony between man and woman, and finally the harmony between the first couple and all creation, comprised the state called *"original justice"*.

The Catechism highlighted the fourfold harmony that constitutes this state of original justice. The harmony of friendship between man and God, the harmony within man himself (his various appetites and reason, even between his soul and body), the harmony between man and woman (or social harmony between human persons), and the harmony between man and the rest of creation.

The *“mastery”* over the world that God offered man in Genesis, was realised above all within man himself: which is the mastery of self.

The first man was unimpaired and ordered in his whole being because he was free from the triple concupiscence that subjugates him to the pleasures of the senses, covetousness for earthly goods, and self-assertion, contrary to the dictates of reason ***(CCC 377)***. In this state of original justice, God furnished our first parents with the potential to remain in ordered harmonies. The lower powers of the soul were held subject to the higher power of reason without any disorder whatsoever. Their bodies also were entirely subject to their souls without bodily defect. Apart from the angels, every other created being was subject to man in original justice. In this state, man, neither suffered nor died. God did not design man to be in a condition of suffering or death. Then, man sinned. As a consequence, he forfeited the fourfold harmony which served to protect against suffering and death.

According to the Catechism ***(CCC 379)***, this entire harmony of original justice, foreseen for man in God's plan was lost by the sin of our first parents. What we witness around us today is thus not the original perfection and harmony of God's creation but a fallen world. It is still a good world, as a matter of speaking, but disharmony now reigns, a disharmony God did <u>not</u> put here. Sin therefore results in the loss of all four harmonies and a disruption of man's intimate friendship with God as man's will has turned away from loving God towards loving other things more than loving his Creator.

The internal integrity that upheld the harmony within man was also lost and the lower appetites were no longer perfectly ordered to man's reason, resulting in concupiscence while man's body was cut off from perfect subjection to man's soul resulting in physical suffering and death. Furthermore, man's perfect harmonious dominion over the rest of creation was similarly lost.

The Creator of all things is perfectly good and perfectly just and perfectly loving. He made all things and saw that they were good. He infused in His creation goodness, original justice and perfect love. The suffering and death that one experiences and witnesses in this life have their origin, hence, not in creation, but in human sin against God our Father. Therefore, blaming God for all the suffering we experience or using our suffering as the premise for arguing against God's existence is man blaming God for what he freely did in disobedience to God. This is a deduction that the atheist would rather soar past than follow through to its logical conclusion.

What purposes does suffering serve?

The answer to this and similar queries draws from the knowledge of God as the One who providentially orchestrates all things in a manner that neither interferes with nor takes away each man's freedom. It follows from this that when God allows one to suffer, He is doing so on the one hand to protect one from a greater evil or on the other hand, to lift one to a greater and outweighing good. There is always a good purpose whenever He allows suffering. This purpose is often inscrutable to us, human beings that we are. Hence the Didache exhorts, *"The workings that befall you receive as good, knowing that apart from God nothing comes to pass"*. In keeping with this wise counsel, we have a choice whenever suffering occurs. We can decide to trust God as our loving Father and receive the discipline of suffering or we can battle against God in distrust and anger as if we know better than He does about what is ultimately good for us.

To grasp the purpose of the suffering that exists in this fallen world, there is the necessity to first clarify why God created man in the first place. God made man to be with Him in eternal, perfect happiness. This is the Beatific Vision that we call Heaven.

It is the perfection of our participation in the divine nature, a participation in the very Life of the Eternal Triune God composing of the immediate, unmediated knowledge of God and the intuitive face-to-face vision of the divine essence. However, with sin, man lost his right to this participation and face-to-face communion thereby introducing into the picture of his existence suffering, evil and death. God allows suffering in this world for a myriad of reasons. What these reasons are can be seen as follows

❖ *To awaken us to reality*

For the purpose of shaking us awake to the fact of our sins, our impending death and judgement, our emptiness apart from God and for the necessity of repentance and return to Himself, God sometimes allows suffering. The parable of the Prodigal son eloquently expresses this purpose. Impoverished and starving in a foreign land, the son's suffering got to the point where he came to his senses in the realisation that things were not as they should be with him. Misery was not supposed to be his portion and cup. His awareness of his misery apart from the embrace of his father helped to evoke in him a desire to return to his father.

Illness and suffering have always been among the gravest problems confronted in human life. In illness, man experiences his powerlessness, his limitations and his finitude.

Every illness can make us glimpse death. Illness can lead to anguish, self-absorption, sometimes even despair and revolt against God. It can also make a person more mature, helping him discern in his life what is not essential so that he can turn toward that which is. Very often illness provokes a search for God and a return to Him ***(CCC 1500-1501)***.

This does not make suffering a 'magic bullet' or a panacea. In response to these sorts of conditions, man can either turn towards God in trust or harden his heart and turn away from God. Even in the fiercest agony and suffering, some still do not turn to God. We see an example in these words from the book of Revelation: *"They were seared by the intense heat and they cursed the name of God, who had control over these plagues, but they refused to repent and glorify Him. The fifth angel poured out his bowl on the throne of the beast, and his kingdom was plunged into darkness. Men gnawed their tongues in agony and cursed the God of heaven because of their pains and their sores, but they refused to repent of what they had done."* ***(Rev. 16:9-11)***.

Thus, God sometimes permits suffering into a man's life to provoke him into searching for Him and to make him realise that this present life is not man's final end but a temporary test in the determination of man's eternal destiny.

❖ *To test us*

We read from the Catechism that:

> God can sometimes seem to be absent and incapable of stopping evil. But in the most mysterious way God the Father has revealed His Almighty Power in the voluntary humiliation and resurrection of His Son, by which he conquered evil. Christ crucified is, thus, *"the power of God and the wisdom of God. For the foolishness of God is wiser than men, and the weakness of God is stronger than men."* It is in Christ's resurrection and exaltation that the Father has shown forth *"the immeasurable greatness of His power in us who believe."* ***(CCC 272)***.

What we see reflected in that portion of the Catechism is the teaching that faith in God the Father Almighty can be put to the test by the experience of evil and suffering. No other example typifies this in the Old Testament like Job. The test of Job provides a view into the larger test that is, this present life. In these tests, we encounter opportunities for us to choose whom we will ultimately serve.

They provide practical demonstrations of the truth of our love for God and can factually distinguish between true love of God and a utilitarian friendship with God that remains true only as long as there is some benefit to be had.

When we, like Job, continue to treasure our friendship with God come what may, we show that this friendship is not one of utility. However, if in response to the removal of life's comforts and luxuries, we turn against God and curse Him, we demonstrate that our love is conditioned by what we get and what He gives us.

- ***To discipline us, to teach us humility and trust, and to work righteousness into us.***

  The Letter to the Hebrews admonishes: *"My son, do not regard lightly the discipline of the Lord, nor be weary when reproved by Him. For the Lord disciplines the one He loves, and chastises every son whom He receives. It is for discipline that you have to endure. God is treating you as sons. For what son is there whom his father does not discipline? If you are left without discipline, in which all have participated, then you are illegitimate children and not sons. Besides this, we have had earthly fathers who disciplined us and we respected them. Shall we not much more be subject to the Father of spirits and live? For they disciplined us for a short time as it seemed best to them, but He disciplines us for our good, that we may share His holiness.*

For the moment all discipline seems painful rather than pleasant, but later it yields the peaceful fruit of righteousness to those who have been trained by it." ***(Heb. 12:5-11)***.

We see the discipline of Jesus Christ whose sorrowful passion dogged his every step all the way to Calvary. He could have died on the *Via Crucis.* He was disciplined to know that his suffering held a purpose, a purpose for which he had to persevere all the way to Calvary where he will die, to wash our sins away and reconcile us back to God Our Father. It always takes discipline to get results.

The Angelic Doctor, St. Thomas Aquinas, in his commentary on this portion of the Bible, says, *"All the saints who have pleased God have gone through many tribulations by which they were made the sons of God"*. We who share with them the title of the sons and daughters of God, through our union with Christ the Son of God, also expect to be disciplined by God our Father. In this communion, we recognise that our loving Father has good reasons for disciplining us no matter how inscrutable these reasons are to us. We are aware that God has valid reasons for permitting our suffering; our response to this suffering is seeking to learn from it and appreciate the lessons therein.

Pope John Paul II carried this further in *Salvifici Doloris*, *"Suffering must serve for conversion, that is, for the rebuilding of goodness in the subject, who can recognise the Divine Mercy in this call to repentance".*

It will however be falling into the exact error of Job's comforters should we assume that all instances of suffering are instances of punishment for specific sins.

The disciples of Jesus also made this mistake of the man who had been blind from birth. They had asked Jesus whose sin resulted in the blindness of the man as it could not be the man since he was born that way. And Jesus answered, *"It was neither that this man sinned, nor his parents; but it was so that the works of God might be displayed in him."* ***(Jn. 9:1-3).***

In another instance of clarifying suffering, Jesus said to those who listened as he preached: *"Do you suppose that these Galileans were greater sinners than all other Galileans because they suffered this fate? I tell you, no, but unless you repent, you will all likewise perish. Or do you suppose that those eighteen on whom the tower in*

*Siloam fell and killed them were worse culprits than all the men who live in Jerusalem? I tell you, no, but unless you repent, you will all likewise perish." **(Lk. 13:1-9)**.*

The Good Teacher was drawing the attention of his audience to the point that the proper response when we hear of the suffering of others is not to consider such persons to be guiltier than those who survived, rather we ought to consider that it was only by God's mercy that we were not among them, so that we may repent and pursue righteousness before our own death.

❖ *To give us the opportunity to love God, to give God glory, to merit glory and to participate in His work of redemption.*

Unlike the atheist whose view of suffering leads inexorably to buttress his argument for the non-existence of God, the Christian perceives suffering as a great gift of God, a gift of mercy by which the sufferer is being led to repentance and eternal life. It is also a gift that makes it apparent to us that God is working some great good in us.

It is the sort of divine gift which lays bare an opportunity to give something great to God in return, just as Christ did in accepting his passion, crucifixion and death. Finally, suffering as such allows us the opportunity to participate in Christ's sufferings and to share in the fellowship of His passion and death.

We see this thought reflected in sections of the New Testament giving evidence of those who took joy in their trials and tribulations.

St. Paul writes in Colossians, *"Now, I rejoice in my sufferings for your sake."* ***(Col. 1:24***).

Acts of the Apostles notes, *"through many tribulations we must enter the Kingdom of God."* ***(Acts 14:22***).

Again in Acts, we see that *"The apostles left the Sanhedrin, rejoicing because they had been counted worthy of suffering disgrace for the Name."* ***(Acts 5:41***).

And in St. Paul's letter to the Romans, we find him make this statement, *"Not only so, but we also rejoice in our sufferings, because we know that suffering produces perseverance; perseverance, character; and character, hope. And hope does not disappoint us, because God has poured out his love into our hearts by the Holy Spirit, whom he has given us."* ***(Rom. 5:3-5***).

This is the exact same mindset we find with the martyrs of the Church. They took joy from their suffering. They never thought for once that suffering was pointless. Unlike the prevalent contemporary perspective which finds nothing worth celebrating in their sufferings as there is no basis for this point-of-view, the Catholic orientation sees things differently. This present world and everything that happens in it is seen from the perspective of the life to come.

Consequently, suffering for Christ here is a great honour from this divine perspective. Thus, when we suffer, our suffering affords us the opportunity of growth in our faith and love for God and also the honour to glorify God in the midst of our trials by loving Him and storing up an incomparable reward in the life to come. Many who knew him will attest that this was clearly the case with Fr. Sylvester Ogbogu.

This all flies in the face of the misleading *"Health and Wealth"* prosperity gospel of today. According to that paradigm, Christ's suffering and cross paid the full price for the salvation of our soul and body. Hence, all Christians have been guaranteed wealth and health in this life. As Christ has done all the suffering required already, there is none left for Christians to carry. Any suffering witnessed among the faithful therefore is a result of demonic presence or generational curses and due to a lack of faith. Herein is observed a logical extension of the error of monergism. Monergistic ideas are founded on the idea that since Christ suffered for us, we do not need to suffer any more.

The redemptive suffering of Jesus Christ cancels out any other suffering for the faithful. It does not recognise the great gift of individual suffering endured with a divine perspective that looks to the life to come and which unites itself with Christ in a participatory process that gives it meaning and significance precisely because it is conjoined with Christ's own sufferings.

In his letter to the Romans, St. Paul captures this when he notes that, *"Now, if we are children, then we are heirs of God and co-heirs with Christ, if indeed we share in His sufferings in order that we may also share in His glory. I consider that our present sufferings are not worth comparing with the glory that will be revealed in us."* ***(Rom. 8:17-18)***.

That is the suffering to which Christ Himself referred when he said, *"If any man would come after me … let him take up his cross daily."* ***(Lk. 9:23***). To the one who so follows, there was the promise from Christ, *"Be faithful, even to the point of death, and I will give you the crown of life."* ***(Rev. 2:10***).

The true meaning of redemptive suffering makes more sense to the one who takes up his cross daily and follows Christ. This is the divine perspective not available to the atheist who thinks only of the meaninglessness of suffering or to the typical modern-day Christian whose opinion of suffering rides solely on the false retribution or recompense idea. Those in the state of grace who embrace the crosses that are given to them in this life earn the promise of eternal reward.

This is another reason we can hope in the eternal tranquillity of Fr. Sylvester with the angels and saints in heaven. St. Paul alluded to this in his second letter to the Thessalonians, *"We ourselves boast of you … for your steadfastness and faith in all your persecutions and in the afflictions, which are enduring." This is evidence of the righteous judgement of God, that you may be made worthy of the Kingdom of God, for which you are suffering* ***(2 Thess. 1:4-5****)*. Pope John Paul II comments on this passage saying, *"Thus to share in the sufferings of Christ is, at the same time, to suffer for the Kingdom of God. In the eyes of the just God, before his judgement, those who share in the suffering of Christ become worthy of this Kingdom. Through their sufferings, in a certain sense they repay the infinite price of the Passion and death of Christ, which became the price of our Redemption."* ***(Salvifici Doloris, n.21)***.

Participating in the sufferings of Christ

In Mystici Corporis Christi, Pope Pius XII noted that *"the salvation of many depends on the prayers and voluntary penances which the members of the Mystical Body of Jesus Christ offer for this intention and on the cooperation of pastors of souls and of the faithful, especially of fathers and mothers of families, a cooperation which they must offer to our Divine Saviour as though they were His associates."* ***(Mystici Corporis Christi, n.44)***.

This extends the salvific and redemptive power of sufferings endured in union with the passion and death of Christ beyond just the benefit of those who endure these sufferings to others. Because we are joined to Christ, our sufferings are joined with His and our endurance of trials and tribulations participates in the Redemption He accomplished.

This does not imply that the work of Christ for our redemption was insufficient. For its purpose, there was nothing more necessary to complete the salvific work of Christ. What is adduced to here is that God has graciously allowed us to participate in that redemptive work, the greatest of all of God's works.

Pope John Paul II expresses it thus:

> *"For, whoever suffers in union with Christ just as the Apostle Paul bears his 'tribulations' in union with Christ, not only receives from Christ that strength already referred to but*

also 'completes' by his suffering 'what is lacking in Christ's afflictions."

The sufferings of Christ created the good of the world's redemption. This good in itself is inexhaustible and infinite. No man can add anything to it. But at the same time, in the mystery of the Church as His Body, Christ has in a sense opened his own redemptive suffering to all human suffering. In so far as man becomes a sharer in Christ's sufferings in any part of the world and at any time in history to that extent he in his own way completes the suffering through which Christ accomplished the Redemption of the world. Does this mean that the Redemption achieved by Christ is not complete? No. it only means that the Redemption, accomplished through satisfactory love, remains always open to all love expressed in human suffering. ***(Salvifici Doloris, n.24).***

There is no one more attuned to this than the mother of Jesus. Mary is the exemplar of suffering in union with Christ, as she was told by Simeon, *"and a sword will pierce even your own soul."* ***(Lk. 2:35)***.

It is consensus of Church Fathers that every suffering Jesus Christ endured in His passion, His mother, who followed all the way, suffered just as much seeing her Son beaten, spat on, fall and persevere to His death on Calvary.

St Paul's words in his letter to the Corinthians ***(1 Cor. 3:9)*** *"For we are God's co-workers"* point to not just St. Paul and the other Apostles but to all of us who are joined to Christ through baptism. By this communion, our sufferings, our trials and our tribulations get to count as participation in Christ's own suffering thereby becoming meaningfully important in the realm of eternity. In Salvifici Doloris, Pope John Paul II alludes to this: *"In bringing about the Redemption through suffering, Christ has also raised human suffering."*

"Thus, each man, in his suffering, can also become a sharer in the redemptive suffering of Christ." ***(Salvifici Doloris, n. 19).***

We make an offering to God of our bodies, our actions, our labour and even our sufferings. St. Paul takes note of this in his writing to the Romans, *"I appeal to you therefore, brethren, by mercies of God, to present your bodies as a living sacrifice, holy and acceptable to God which is your spiritual worship."* ***(Rm.12:1)***. We make this offering of our lives and sufferings formally in the Mass when we consciously offer ourselves up with our sufferings along with Christ to God the Father during the Offertory.

In an informal manner, we can, whenever we suffer, *"offer it up"* simply by asking God to join our suffering to Christ's and to use our suffering in the salvific work of Christ. It is the consolation of all who know Fr. Sylvester that he willingly offered his tribulations and trials from his illness to the Father to participate in Christ's redemptive work.

Response to suffering?

When we experience suffering from the divine perspective and join our sufferings to God, we clear our minds to efficaciously respond in ways that to many without the same perspective as ours will appear folly. But we know that we fulfil our baptismal responsibilities of participating as true sons and daughters of God in the redemptive work of Christ. It is out of the ordinary for any human being to pray for suffering. However, whether one prays for suffering or not, they come. These are some of the many ways our response to our trials can transform our tribulations (all with their scriptural attributions):

- The story of Job presents us with the path to a more potent response to any and all the sufferings, trials, and tribulations that we encounter in this fallen world. He responded by worshipping God. *"Then Job arose and tore his robe and shaved his head, and fell to the ground and worshipped. He said, 'Naked I came from my mother's womb, and naked shall I return there. The Lord gave and the Lord has taken away; blessed be the name of the Lord.' Through all this, Job did not sin nor did he blame God."* ***(Job 1:20-22)***.
- By offering our sufferings up to God: *"Is anyone among you suffering? Then, he must pray."* ***(James 5:13)***.
- By giving thanks: *"In everything give thanks; for this is God's will for you in Christ Jesus."* ***(1 Thess. 5:18)***.
- By rejoicing that we have been counted worthy to suffer for Christ: *"Now, I rejoice in my sufferings for your sake."* ***(Col. 1:24)***.
- By looking to the example of Jesus Christ Himself, who suffered for us to demonstrate to us both the magnitude of our sin and the greater magnitude of His infinite love for us. "He also says, *'Shall I not drink the cup which the Father has given me?'"* ***(John 18:11)***.

Christ received the cup of suffering from His Father, in humble obedience, and in doing so perfectly demonstrated His love for the Father. *"My Father, if it be possible, let this cup pass from me; nevertheless, not as I will, but as thou wilt", … "My Father, if this cannot pass unless I drink it, thy will be done."* ***(Matt. 26:39,42)***.

- By looking to the return of Jesus Christ and the life to come. We see St. Peter counsel us in this: *"Fix your hope completely on the grace to be brought to you at the revelation of Jesus Christ."* ***(1 Pet. 1:13).*** For then, *"… there will no longer be any death; there will no longer be any mourning, or crying, or pain; the first things have passed away."* ***(Rev. 21:4).***
- By trusting in the unfailing word of God, Jesus made a declarative statement in ***(Jn 16:33)*** that, *"in the world you will have many tribulations but do not be afraid, for I have overcome the world."*

Is it not relieving to know that these characterise the days that the amiable Fr. Sylvester spent while enduring the conditions his illness brought upon him? Charles Albert Tindley in the lyrics of his piece titled *"We Will Understand it Better By and By"* instructively says:

1. *We are tossed and driven on the restless sea of time;*
   Sombre skies and howling tempests oft succeed a bright sunshine;
   In that land of perfect day, when the mists have rolled away,
   We will understand it better by and by.
   Refrain
   By and by, when the morning comes,
   When the saints of God are gathered home,
   We'll tell the story how we've overcome, For we'll understand it better by and by.
2. *We are often destitute of the things that life demands,*
   Want of food and want of shelter, thirsty hills and barren lands;
   We are trusting in the Lord, and according to God's Word, We will understand it better by and by.
3. *Trials dark on every hand, and we cannot understand*
   All the ways that God could lead us to that bless'd promised land;
   But He guides us with His eye, and we'll follow till we die,
   For we'll understand it better by and by.
4. *Temptations, hidden snares often take us unawares,*
   And our hearts are made to bleed for a thoughtless word or deed;

And we wonder why the test when we try to do our best,
But we'll understand it better by and by.

Chapter Four

Final Words

Illness and suffering feature among the gravest afflictions that confront human beings and imperil human life. Under the pain of illness, man experiences his powerlessness, his limitations and, ultimately, his finitude. Every illness, thus affords one a glimpse of death. It comes with anguish leading to self-absorption, sometimes despair and, in the extreme case, revolt against God. It can conversely open a person's eyes, making him more mature, helping him discern in his life, what is essential and giving him the necessity to turn towards that which is essential. It so happens that often, sickness provokes a search for God and a determination to return to Him ***(cf. Catechism of the Catholic Church 1997)***.

This return to God can open the sufferer's eyes to the redemptive and salvific understanding of suffering. Each person is called to share in that suffering which brought about our redemption. Christ's call to us to take up our cross is expressly answered when the one who suffers the tribulations of ill health understands his suffering as partaking in this mission. He shares in that suffering through which all human suffering has also been redeemed.

Pope John Paul II in Salvifici Doloris asserts that by his passion, Christ raised human suffering to the level of the Redemption. Thus, each man, in his suffering can also become a sharer in the redemptive suffering of Christ. This is what Fr. Sylvester became; a sharer in Christ's redemptive suffering and an example for those who shared of his life.

Although victory over sin and death was achieved by Christ's resurrection, Pope John Paul II ***(Salvifici Doloris)*** notes, that victory did not abolish the temporal suffering from human life nor did it free from suffering the whole historical dimension of human existence. Yet, it throws a new light upon this dimension and upon every form of tribulation. This is the light of salvation. It was this teaching that Rev Fr. Sylvester Ogbogu personified in the period of his illness up to the moment, during the celebration of the suffering, passion and death of our Lord in Holy Week, when he returned to his Maker.

Nuggets of wisdom

"A true Christian is proved in the fire of tribulation."

Amorth

*****

"If when we are ill, our recovery will contribute to the glory of God and the good of our soul, he who healed so many when he was on earth, will certainly heal us. If, on the contrary, the illness is more advantageous to us, he will instead give us the strength to suffer."

St. Alphonsus Liguori

*****

"Whether pleasant or painful, the present does not last forever."

St. Alphonsus Liguori

*****

"Sorrow is given to us on purpose to cure us of sin."

St. Anthony Mary Claret

"But different kinds of sufferings are imposed on us to test and prove us, and many forms of temptations are inflicted upon us by loss of wealth, burning fevers, torments of wounds, by the death of dear ones.

Nothing else distinguishes the unjust and the just more than this, that in adversities the unjust man complains and blasphemes because of impatience, while the just man is proved by patience, as it is written:

"In thy sorrow endure and, in thy humiliation, keep patience, for gold and silver are tried in fire."

St. Basil

*****

"God suffereth not His servants to be afflicted save for their good."

St. Augustine

*****

"He sends us crosses, not because He wishes evil to us, but because he desires our welfare, and because he knows that they are conducive to our salvation."

St. Bonaventure

"In the same way that a powerful medicine cures an illness, so illness itself is a medicine to cure passion. And there is much profit of soul in bearing illness quietly and giving thanks to God."

St. Cardinal Newman

*****

"If troubled by poverty, by sickness, by persecution, or afflictions and anxieties of any sort, let us be convinced that none of these things can happen to us without the permission of God, who is the supreme Arbiter of all things.

We should, therefore, not suffer our minds to be too much disturbed by them, but bear up against them with fortitude, having always on our lips the words: The will of the Lord be done; and also those of holy Job, As it hath pleased the Lord, so it is done: blessed be the name of the Lord."

St. Colette

*****

"Let them not, however, lose heart; to face bitter combats is a mark of Christians, and to endure grave labours to the end is a mark of them who, as good soldiers of Christ, follow Him closely."

St. Cyprian

"Follow the Divine Master up the steep slope of Calvary, loaded with the cross and when it pleases Him to place us on the cross by confining us to a bed of pain, let us thank Him and consider ourselves lucky to be honoured in this way, aware that to be on the cross with Jesus is infinitely more perfect than merely contemplating Him on the cross."

St. Francis of Assisi

*****

"This, in short, is the difference between us and others who know not God, that in misfortune they complain and murmur, while adversity does not call us away from the truth of virtue and faith, but strengthens us by its suffering."

St. Francis de Sales

*****

"Pain and sorrow are the almost necessary medicines of the rashness of nature. Without these, men are like spoilt children; they act as if they considered everything must give way to their own wishes and conveniences."

- St. Francis Xavier

"There the greater shall be our joy; the more we have suffered here below."

St John of Avila

*****

"It is only by sacrifice and suffering, offered as penance, that you will be able, by the grace of God, to convert sinners."

St. John Chrysostom

*****

"To thank God in all things that are agreeable to us, is acceptable to Him, but to accept with cheerfulness that which is repugnant to our inclinations, is still more pleasing to Him. Father M. Avila used to say, that 'a single blessed be God, in adversity, is better than six thousand thanksgivings in prosperity."

St. John Vianney

*****

"If there be a true way that leads to the Everlasting Kingdom, it is most certainly that of suffering, patiently endured."

St. Louis IX

"Then Jesus said to his disciples, 'Whoever wishes to come after me, must deny himself, take up his cross, and follow me.'"

Mt 16:24

*****

"Whoever does not carry his own cross and come after me cannot be my disciple."

- LK 14:27

*****

"Great indeed are the advantages of tribulations. The Lord sends them to us not because he wishes our misfortune, but because he desires our welfare. Hence, when they come upon us, we must embrace them with thanksgiving, and must not only resign ourselves to the divine will, but must also rejoice that God treats us as he treated his son Jesus Christ, whose life upon this Earth was always full of tribulation."

St. Padre Pio of Pietrelcina

*****

"There is no doubt that suffering is the greatest trial against our faith; it causes us either to lose it or strengthen it."

Pope St. Gregory

"The jewels which give the greatest splendour to the crown of the saints in Heaven, are the tribulations which they bore with patience, as coming from the hands of the Lord."

St. Pachomius

*****

"What do you think the bed of tribulation is? It is simply the school of humility."

Pope St. John Paul II

*****

"I am fed upon the bread of tribulation and the water of affliction but nevertheless, I have not given up, and I will not give up, doing my duty."

St. Robert Soutwell

*****

"Oh my God, how good thou art. Thou does use the very sickness of man's body to heal the soul."

St. Syncletice

*****

"In sending us tribulations, God intends to make us saints."

St. Vincent de Paul

"As in Heaven, nothing will be sweeter than to resemble Him in His glory, so here on earth, nothing is more to our advantage than to be like Him in His Passion.

We must remember that all incapacity and distress is sent to us by God. Life and death, health and sickness, are all ordered by Him; and in whatever form they come, it is always to help us and for our good."

- St. Teresa of Avila

Tribute

Fr. Sylvester, so many thoughts come to my mind whenever I remember you. You were my priest, friend, mentor and always wanted the best for me. You were a perfect example of a good priest, someone who was always ready to go out of your way to help others, be it your fellow priests and even the lay people. Your smiles and personality made people feel very comfortable around you and you were so protective of your loved ones.

I was gobsmacked when I got the news that you were ill and having learnt that it was cancer, made me sick to my stomach and I remember screaming, ***"GOD, WHY?"*** I had so much faith and hope through my prayers for you that you were going to come out of it, but God had a greater plan for you. I remember visiting you at the hospital and you looked so cheerful as usual with smiles all over your face and you even asked me to share in your dinner with you.

When I asked you to carry on eating, your response was, ***"You don't know what delicious meal you are missing out on."***

You were so much into sports that you did not allow your health to deter you from the things you loved, than even whilst on your hospital bed with no television to watch, you were eager to know what the scores were, even when you were at your lowest moments. I will always choose you over and over again as a friend even if it means losing you again, it is worth all the tears in the world.

Your demise has left a deep hole in my heart and in the hearts of all those who were privileged to come into contact with you. On 28th March 2018, you left this sinful world and your lovely family and friends to be with the Lord. That day will never be forgotten. Years will come and go but your memories will linger on. Saying goodbye Fr. Sly is never an easy thing, but I know in my heart that you are finally pain-free and happy. I am more than grateful to God for having the chance to meet you, crack jokes and laugh with you once more before your departure. My only consolation is that you are with the angels and saints in heaven, and you left this earth during the most important times in the church's calendar - HOLY WEEK.

Adieu my mentor Fr. Sylvester.

About the Author

Chioma Okolia is a British Nigerian who currently lives in London. She is an Information Technology expert who has worked with different organisations within the United Kingdom. Chioma obtained a BSc in Information and Communications Technology from the University of Greenwich, and a Certificate in Information Technology and programming from the Association of Computer Professionals.

Her work experience coupled with her love for meeting people and travelling has taken her to countries within Europe and America creating platforms for her to work with different persons at different levels and to encounter people at different stages of life.

She engaged Fr. Sylvester on various topics including human suffering, and so she feels persuaded to share some thoughts on the reality of human suffering. She presently lives in the United Kingdom.

Reference Materials

Catechism of the Catholic Church 1997. 2nd ed Vatican City:

Libreria Editrice Vaticana;

Http://www.vatican.va/archive/ENG0015/_index.htm.

Catholic Bishops' Conference of Philippines 1997.

Catechism for Filipino Catholics. Manila, Philippines:

ECCCE Word & Life Publications.

Bryan C. A Catholic Reflection on the Meaning of Suffering.

Http://www.calledtocommunion.com/2009/08/a-catholic-reflection-on-the-meaining-of-Suffering/#identifier_64_2208.

Viktor F.E. 2006. Man's search for meaning. Boston:

Beacon Press.

Pope Pius XII, 1943. Mystici Corporis, On the Church as the

Mystical Body of Christ,

https://www.catholicculture.org

Pope John Paul II. 1984. Salvifici doloris, On the Christian

Meaning of human suffering

http://w2.vatican.ca/content/john-paul-ii/en/apost_letters/1984/documents/hf_jp-li_apl_110211984_salvifici-doloris.html

The Pope John Paul II. 2000. Address to the 18 International

Congress of the Transplantation Society

http://w2.Vatican.va/content/john-paulli_spe_20000829_transplants.html

Tribute to Sylvester OGBOGU, SMA, 1972 - 2018.

Https://mansly.muchloved.com

Printed in Dunstable, United Kingdom

66205826R00048